*Taittiriya Upanishad
and Commentary*

By
Charles Johnston

Copyright © 2021 Lamp of Trismegistus. All rights reserved. No part of this publication may be reproduced or transmitted in any form or by any means, electronic or mechanical, including photocopying, recording, or by any information storage and retrieval system, without permission in writing from Lamp of Trismegistus. Reviewers may quote brief passages.

ISBN: 978-1-63118-538-0

Esoteric Classics:
Eastern Studies

Other Books in this Series and Related Titles

Isha Upanishad and Commentary by Charles Johnston (978-1-63118-490-1)

Kena Upanishad and Commentary by Charles Johnston (978-1-63118-491-8)

Katha Upanishad and Commentary by Charles Johnston (978-1-63118-493-2)

Prashna Upanishad and Commentary by Charles Johnston (978-1-63118-494-9)

Mandukya Upanishad and Commentary by Charles Johnston (978-1-63118-497-0)

Mundaka Upanishad and Commentary by Charles Johnston (978-1-63118-496-3)

Atma Bodha & Tattva Bodha by Adi Shankara &c (978-1-63118-401-7)

The Crest-Jewel of Wisdom by Adi Shankara (978-1-63118-475-8)

Yoga Sutras of Patanjali and Commentary by Charles Johnston (978-1-63118-536-6)

The Book of Wisdom of Solomon by King Solomon (978-1-63118-502-1)

Catholicism, Yoga and Hinduism by Hartmann &c (978-1-63118-478-9)

Yoga, Hatha-Yoga and Raja-Yoga by Annie Besant (978-1-63118-476-5)

The Tree of Wisdom by Nagarjuna (978-1-63118-470-3)

The Path of Light: A Manual of Maha-Yana Buddhism (978-1-63118-471-0)

Buddhist Psalms by Shinran (978-1-63118-465-9)

Tao Te Ching & Commentary by Lao Tzu & C Johnston (978-1-63118-495-6)

The Hymns of Hermes by G. R. S. Mead (978-1-63118-405-5)

The Golden Verses of Pythagoras: Five Translations (978-1-63118-479-6)

Gnosis of the Mind by G. R. S. Mead (978-1-63118-408-6)

The Hymn of Jesus by G. R. S. Mead (978-1-63118-492-5)

The Book of the Watchers by Enoch (978-1-63118-416-1)

Audio versions are also available on Audible, Amazon and Apple

Other Books in this Series and Related Titles

Alchemy in the Nineteenth Century by Helena P. Blavatsky (978-1-63118-446-8)

The Influence of Pythagoras on Freemasonry and Other Essays (978-1-63118-404-8)

The Mysteries of Freemasonry & the Druids by A Mackey &c (978-1-63118-444-4)

The Rosicrucian Chemical Marriage by Christian Rosenkreuz (978-1-63118-458-1)

Ancient Mysteries and Secret Societies by M P Hall (978-1-63118-410-9)

Masonic and Rosicrucian History by M P Hall & H Voorhis (978-1-63118-486-4)

History, Analysis and Secret Tradition of the Tarot by Hall &c (978-1-63118-445-1)

Essays on the Esoteric Tradition of Karma by A Besant &c (978-1-63118-426-0)

The Hidden Mysteries of Christianity by Annie Besant (978–1–63118–534–2)

The Secrets of Enoch by Enoch (978-1-63118-449-9)

Crystal Vision Through Crystal Gazing by Frater Achad (978-1-63118-455-0)

The Historic, Mythic and Mystic Christ by Annie Besant (978-1-63118-533-5)

The Human Aura: Astral Colors and Thought Forms (978-1-63118-419-2)

The Master Mason's Handbook by J S M Ward (978-1-63118-474-1)

Rosicrucian Rules, Secret Signs, Codes and Symbols by various (978-1-63118-488-8)

An Outline of Theosophy by C W Leadbeater (978-1-63118-452-9)

Cloud Upon the Sanctuary by A E Waite & K Eckartshausen (978-1-63118-438-3)

The Feminine Occult by various authors (978-1-63118-711-7)

Magical Essays and Instructions by Florence Farr (978-1-63118-418-5)

Paracelsus, the Four Elements and Their Spirits by M P Hall (978-1-63118-400-0)

Arcane Formulas or Mental Alchemy by W W Atkinson (978-1-63118-459-8)

Audio versions are also available on Audible, Amazon and Apple

Table of Contents

Introduction…7

Taittiriya Upanishad
Instructions for Disciples
Translated by Charles Johnston…9

Taittiriya Upanishad
Secondary Translation & Commentary
By Charles Johnston…30

INTRODUCTION

The word "esoteric" can be difficult to define. Esotericism in general can be seen less as a system of beliefs and more as a category, which encompasses numerous, different systems of beliefs. It's a bit of juxtaposition, since the word "esoteric" indicates something that few people know about, while the term itself broadly covers numerous philosophies, practices, areas of study and belief systems.

In a greater sense, Esotericism acts as a storehouse for secret knowledge, which is often considered ancient *(by tradition, if not by fact),* passed down from generation to generation, in private. At various times in history, simply possessing the knowledge of some of these subjects, was considered illegal and a jailable offence, if discovered. This usually included such general topics as Alchemy, Pharmacology, Qabalah, Hermeticism, Occultism, Ceremonial Magic, Astrology, Divination, Rosicrucianism and so on. Collectively, these areas of study were often referred to as the esoteric sciences.

Sometimes, the outer garment of a subject isn't esoteric, while what is hidden beneath it, is. As an example, Freemasonry isn't necessarily esoteric by nature (at *least not anymore),* but certain signs, passwords and handshakes given to the candidate during their initiation, are in fact, esoteric, in the sense that they are hidden from the general public.

Today, in the twenty-first century, such topics are readily available at bookstores across the country, and numerous mainsteam publishers offer beginners guides and coffee-table volumes on many of these subjects, intended for mass appeal. Books like *"The Secret"* have turned previously arcane topics into household knowledge. All that being the case, however, it isn't to say that there still aren't buried secrets to uncover, ancient wisdom being ignored and forgotten mysteries to be explored. In fact, it is often that we are only able to further our own studies by standing on the shoulders of these disappearing giants.

Lamp of Trismegistus is doing its part to help preserve humanity's esoteric history by making some of these classics available to those students who are seeking to unearth the knowledge of these ancient colossi.

So, be sure to check other titles from our *Esoteric Classics* series, as well as our *Occult Fiction, Theosophical Classics, Eastern Studies, Foundations of Freemasonry Series, Supernatural Fiction, Paranormal Research Series, Studies in Buddhism* and our *Christian Apocrypha Series.* You can also download the audio versions of most of these titles from Amazon, Apple or Audible, for learning on the go.

TAITTIRIYA UPANISHAD

Translated by Charles Johnston

INSTRUCTIONS FOR DISCIPLES

I

The Taittiriya Upanishad is made up, for the most part, of Instructions for younger disciples, who are learning the first lessons of the secret wisdom from a Master.

As might be expected, these Instructions are often enigmatic, in part because of their brevity; they are intended, not simply to convey information to the mind, but rather to awaken the intuition and to supply material for careful, deliberative thought and meditation.

They contain, among other things, tables of Correspondences, illustrating what *The Secret Doctrine* calls "the eternal law of correspondences and analogy," regarding which it is further said:

"From Gods to men, from Worlds to atoms, from a Star to a rushlight, from the Sun to the vital heat of the meanest organic being—the world of Form and Existence is an immense chain, the links of which are all connected. The Law of Analogy is the first key to the world-problem, and these links have to be studied co-ordinately in their Occult relation to each other" (S.D., I, pages 640 and 662).

To illustrate the method of study: If the section entitled "The Law of Correspondences" be drawn up as a table, it will be found that the disciple is compared with the father, the Master being the mother; the purpose of the teaching is, to bring forth the "new creature," the spiritual man, in the disciple. Thoughtful study will reveal many points of equal interest.

Invocation

May Mitra, divinity of the day, guard us! May Varuna, divinity of the night, guard us! May Aryaman, divinity of the sun, guard us! May Indra, divinity of power, guard us! May Brihaspati, divinity of voice and of intelligence, guard us! May wide-striding Vishnu, divinity of progress, guard us!

Obeisance to the Eternal! Obeisance to thee, Vayu, the Great Breath! Thou, verily, art the Eternal made manifest! Thee, verily, as the Eternal made manifest I shall declare. I shall declare the Truth. I shall declare the Real. May it protect me! May it protect the speaker! May it protect me! May it protect the speaker! Om: Peace! Peace! Peace!

Intoning Sacred Sentences

Om: We shall set forth in order the teaching regarding Intoning.

The colour of the sound; the tone, whether high or low; the measure, whether long or short; the stress, whether strong or light; the enunciation, making the sound audible; the combination, linking sounds together.

Thus the teaching of Intoning is declared.

The Law of Correspondences

May honour abide with us two, Master and disciple! May the radiance of the Eternal abide with us two!

We shall now set forth in order the secret teaching of Correspondences, under five heads: Regarding the world; the givers of light; the teaching; offspring; self. This is called the teaching of Correspondences.

Now, regarding the world: the earth is the initial form, heaven is the final form; the ether of space is the mediating power; Vayu, the Great Breath, brings about the union. Thus, regarding the world.

Now, regarding the givers of light: fire is the initial form; the sun is the final form; the waters of space are the mediating power; the lightning brings about the union. Thus, regarding the givers of light.

Now, regarding the teaching: the Master is the initial form; the accepted disciple is the final form; the secret teaching is the mediating power; the imparting of the teaching brings about the union. Thus, regarding the teaching.

Now, regarding offspring: the mother is the initial form; the father is the final form; the offspring is the mediating power; the engendering brings about the union. Thus, regarding offspring.

Now, regarding self: the lower jaw is the initial form; the upper jaw is the final form; voice is the mediating power; the tongue brings about the union. Thus, regarding self.

These are the Correspondences. He who knows these Correspondences, thus set forth in order, is united with offspring and flocks, with the radiance of the Eternal, with food and all blessings, with the heavenly world.

Invocation by the Master

The Power who inspired the sacred hymns is the Divinity of universal form. Above the hymns, he came into being from the Everlasting. May this Ruler endow me with holy wisdom! May I, O Radiant One, become a container and bestower of immortality!

May my body be full of vigour! May my tongue be sweeter than honey! May I hear fully with my ears!

Thou art the vesture of the Eternal, endowed with holy wisdom! Guard for me what I have heard!

Divine Grace brings blessings, and distributes them. May that Grace take to herself these vestures and herds! May she provide food and drink, granting me a blessing always! May she grant the flocks with their fleeces! Adoration!

May disciples, serving the Eternal, come to me! Adoration!

May disciples, serving the Eternal, come apart to me! Adoration!

May disciples, serving the Eternal, come forth to me! Adoration!

May disciples, serving the Eternal, conquer themselves! Adoration!

May disciples, serving the Eternal, win peace! Adoration!

May I be Radiance among mankind! Adoration!

May I be more blessed than those rich in possessions! Adoration!

May I enter, Lord, into Thee! Adoration!

Thou, Lord, enter into me! Adoration!

In the Power, thousand-rayed, in Thee, Lord, I am clean! Adoration!

As waters flow, descending; as the months flow into the sum of days, so, Universal Lord, let disciples, serving the Eternal, come from the whole world to me! Adoration!

Thou art my Refuge! Pour thy Light upon me! Come to me!

The Four Realms

Earth, Mid-world, Heaven: These are the three Expressions. Mahachamasya made known a fourth, in addition to these: the Great One. This is the Eternal, this is the Supreme Self. The other divine powers are its members.

The Earth, verily, is this world; the Mid-world is the interspace; Heaven is that world; the Great One is the sun. Through the sun, verily, all worlds are made great.

The Earth, verily, is this fire; the mid-world is the wind; Heaven is the sun; the Great One is the moon. Through the moon, verily all lights are made great.

The Earth, verily, is the Rig Veda; the Mid-world is the Sama Veda; Heaven is the Yajur Veda; the Great One is knowledge of the Eternal. Through knowledge of the Eternal, all the Vedas are made great.

The Earth, verily, is the forward-breath; the Mid-world is the downward-breath; Heaven is the distributive-breath; the Great One is food. Through food, verily, all the vital breaths are made great.

They, verily, these four, are divided fourfold. The Expressions are four and four. Who knows these, knows the Eternal; to him all the bright Powers bring victory.

The Man Formed of Mind

This radiant ether, here, in the heart within, in it is the Spiritual Man, formed of Mind, immortal, of the colour of gold; here, at the division of the palate, this, which is pendent, like a nipple, this is the womb of the Ruler. Opening a way here, at the top of the head, where the hair separates, and saying, Earth! he establishes himself on this fire; saying, Mid-world! he establishes himself upon the wind; saying, Heaven! He establishes himself in the sun; saying, the Great One! he establishes himself in the Eternal. He wins self-mastery. He wins the Lord of the mind. He becomes lord of voice, lord of vision, lord of hearing, lord of knowledge, all this, he becomes, and more, the Eternal, whose vesture is the ether of space, whose soul is the Real, whose garden is Life, whose joy is Mind, whose treasure is Peace immortal. Thus worship, thou of the ancient Yoga!

Fivefold Correspondences

Earth	interspace	heaven	directions	inter-directions
Fire	wind	sun	moon	constellations
Water	plants	trees	space	self

Thus, with regard to beings. Now, with regard to self:

Forward-breath	distributive-breath	downward-breath	upward-breath	uniting-breath
Vision	hearing	mind	voice	touch
Skin	flesh	sinew	bone	marrow

Thus distributing the powers, a Seer and Sage has said: Fivefold, verily, is this all. Through the five, he wins the five.

The Sacred Syllable OM

Om is the eternal. Om is all this universe. Om is also the expression of assent. Saying, Om! Invoke! they invoke at the sacrifice. Saying, Om! they intone the Sama hymns. Saying, Om! they praise the weapons. Saying, Om! the priest utters the response. Saying, Om! the chief priest chants the opening praise. Saying, Om! the sacrificer assents to the fire-oblation. Saying, Om I the Brahman, about to recite, prays, May I receive inspiration! He receives inspiration.

Study and Instruction

The True, study and instruction; the Real, study and instruction; fervour, study and instruction; control, study and instruction; peace, study and instruction; the fires, study and instruction; the fire-oblation, study and instruction; guests, study and instruction; the sons of man, study and instruction; offspring, study and instruction; engendering, study and instruction; bringing up children, study and instruction.

The true!" said Rathitara, speaker of truth. "Fervour!" said Paurushishti, ever fervent. "Study and instruction!" said Naka, son of Mudgala, "for this is fervour, this is fervour!"

A Meditation

I am he who fells the tree of rebirth; my glory is as a mountain peak, exalted, pure; I am as the nectar in the sun, the treasure, radiant; I am the possessor of wisdom, immortal, indestructible!

Master and Disciple

When he has taught him the Vedas, the Master thus instructs the accepted disciple:

Speak the truth! Work righteousness! Be not remiss in study! Bring a gift acceptable to thy Master, and break not the link of spiritual descent! Depart not from the truth! Depart not from righteousness! Depart not from true welfare! Depart not from true prosperity! Depart not from study and from thy instruction!

Depart not from what is owed to the bright Powers and the Fathers! Let thy mother be to thee as a divinity! Let thy father be to thee as a divinity! Let thy Master be to thee as a divinity! Let a guest be to thee as a divinity! Let all blameless works be performed, but not others! Those things which are esteemed good among us, should be revered by thee, and not others! Whichever knowers of the Eternal are best among us, should be received by thee with reverence!

Give thy gifts with faith! Give not without faith! Give with grace! Give with humility! Give with reverence! Give with compassion!

If thou shouldest have a doubt concerning thy work, or concerning conduct, whatever knowers of the Eternal are there, full of judgment, qualified, devoted, gentle-hearted, loving righteousness, as these shall bear themselves in such a matter, so do thou bear thyself!

Concerning those who are reprimanded, whatever knowers of the Eternal are there, full of judgment, qualified, devoted, gentle-hearted, loving righteousness, as these shall bear themselves in such a matter, so do thou bear thyself! This is the instruction, this is the counsel, this is the secret wisdom of the Vedas, this is the command handed down; thus shalt thou reverently serve! Thus, verily, should service be rendered.

Closing Invocation

May Mitra, divinity of the day, guard us! May Varuna, divinity of the night, guard us! May Aryaman, divinity of the sun, guard us! May Indra, divinity of power, guard us! May Brihaspati, divinity of voice and of intelligence, guard us! May wide-striding Vishnu, divinity of progress, guard us!

Obeisance to the Eternal! Obeisance to thee, Vayu, the Great Breath!

Thou, verily, art the Eternal made manifest! Thee, verily, as the Eternal made manifest, I have declared. I have declared the Truth. I have declared the Real. It has protected me. It has protected the speaker. Om: Peace! Peace! Peace!

II

He who knows the Eternal attains to the Supreme. Therefore, this has been declared: He who has gained the knowledge of the Eternal, the Truth, Wisdom, Infinite, hid in the secret place, in the highest shining ether, he, indeed, gains all desires together with the All-Wise Eternal.

From That, verily, from this universal Self, the shining Ether came to birth; from Ether, the Wind, the Great Breath; from the Wind, Fire; from Fire, the Waters; from the Waters, the Earth; from the Earth, Plants; from Plants, Food; from Food, the Seed; from the Seed, Man. So, verily, this man is formed of the essence of food; this is his head, this is his right side, this is his left side, this is himself, this is the basis whereon he stands firm. Therefore, there is this verse:

From food, verily, beings are born, whatsoever they are that dwell on earth; and so by food they live, and so to it they go at the end; for food is the eldest of beings, therefore it is called the all-healing; they, verily, obtain all food, who worship the Eternal as food. Food, verily, is the eldest of beings, therefore it is called the all-healing. From food, beings are born; born, through food they increase; That is eaten, and eats beings, therefore it is called food.

Within him, within this formed of the essence of food, there is another inner self, formed of life-breath; by it, this is filled. And he, verily, has the form of man; according to the human form of that, this has the form of man; the forward-breath is his head, the distributive-breath is his right side, the downward-breath is his left side, the ether is himself, earth is the basis whereon he stands firm. Therefore, there is this verse:

With breath the bright powers breathe, and men and beasts, whatsoever they be, for breath is of beings the life; therefore it is called all-life; they, verily, gain a complete life, who worship the Eternal as the life-breath. For breath is the life of all beings, therefore it is called all-life. This self is embodied in the other, the preceding.

Within him, within this formed of life-breath, there is another inner self, formed of mind; by it, this is filled. And he, verily, has the form of man; according to the human form of that, this has the form of man; the Yajur is his head, the Rig is his right side, the Sama is his left side, the instruction is himself, Atharva and Angiras are the basis whereon he stands firm. Therefore, there is this verse:

That from which words turn back, falling short, together with mind, knowing that bliss of the Eternal, he fears no more for ever. This self is embodied in the other, the preceding.

Within him, within this formed of mind, there is another inner self, formed of understanding; by it, this is filled. And he, verily, has the form of man; according to the human form of that, this has the form of man; faith is his head, righteousness is his right side, truth is his left side, union is himself, the mighty is the basis whereon he stands firm. Therefore, there is this verse:

Understanding draws forth sacrifice, and draws forth works also; as understanding, all the bright powers worship the Eternal, the eldest. If he has come to know the Eternal as understanding, and is not allured therefrom, putting away sins with the body, he gains all desires. This self is embodied in the other, the preceding.

Within him, within this formed of understanding, there is another inner self, formed of bliss; by it, this is filled. And he, verily, has the form of man; according to the human form of that, this has the form of man; love is his head, joy is his right side, rejoicing is his left side, bliss is himself, the Eternal is the basis whereon he stands firm. Therefore, there is this verse:

Unmanifest, verily, he becomes, if he knows the Eternal as unmanifest. If he knows that the Eternal is, thereafter they know him as manifest. This self is embodied in the other, the preceding.

And so there are the further questions: whether anyone who has not attained to wisdom gains that world on going forth, or whether he who has attained to wisdom gains that world on going forth.

He desired: may I become many, may I form beings. He brooded with fervour; brooding with fervour, he emanated all this, whatsoever there is; when he had emanated it, following, he entered into it; entering it, he became what is here and what is there, the defined and the undefined, that which has form and what is formless, understanding and what is beyond understanding, both the real and the unreal. As the real, he became whatsoever is here; that is called the real. Therefore, there is this verse:

Unmanifest, verily, was That in the beginning; from That, verily, the manifest came into being; That manifested itself as the Self, therefore That is called the Self-formed. That, verily, which is Self-formed, is the essence; gaining that essence, he possesses bliss; for who could live, who could breathe, if the shining ether were not joy? For this, verily, brings joy. For when he finds the fearless, the firm foundation, in that which is invisible, selfless, undefined, formless, then, verily, he has gained that which is beyond fear. But if he makes separateness in this, then fear is his. But That, verily, is the fear of him who has gained wisdom and understanding. Therefore, there is this verse:

From awe of That, the wind blows; from awe of That, the sun rises; from awe of That, the Fire-lord and the Sky-lord, and Death runs as the fifth.

This is the measuring of joy:

Let there be a youth, a righteous youth, who has mastered the teaching, very swift, very firm, very powerful, and let this whole earth be full of riches for him; this is one joy of the sons of men.

A hundred joys of the sons of men are one joy of the angels of human form, and of the disciple who has attained, who is not stricken by desire.

A hundred joys of the angels of human form are one joy of the angels of divine form, and of the disciple who has attained, who is not stricken by desire.

A hundred joys of the angels of divine form are one joy of the Fathers, in the long-enduring worlds, and of the disciple who has attained, who is not stricken by desire.

A hundred joys of the Fathers in the long-enduring worlds are one joy of the beings divine by birth, and of the disciple who has attained, who is not stricken by desire.

A hundred joys of the beings divine by birth are one joy of those divine beings who have gained divinity through work, and of the disciple who has attained, who is not stricken by desire.

A hundred joys of those divine beings who have gained divinity through work are one joy of the divinities, and of the disciple who has attained, who is not stricken by desire.

A hundred joys of the divinities are one joy of the Lord of heaven, and of the disciple who has attained, who is not stricken by desire.

A hundred joys of the Lord of heaven are one joy of the Instructor of divine beings, and of the disciple who has attained, who is not stricken by desire.

A hundred joys of the Instructor of divine beings are one joy of the Father of all beings, and of the disciple who has attained, who is not stricken by desire.

A hundred joys of the Father of all beings are one joy of the Eternal, and of the disciple who has attained, who is not stricken by desire.

He who is here, in man, and he who is there, in the sun, are one. He who knows this, on going forth from this world transcends this self formed of food, transcends this self formed of life-breath, transcends this self formed of mind, transcends this self formed of understanding, transcends this self formed of bliss. Therefore, then: is this verse:

That from which words turn back, falling short, together with mind, knowing that bliss of the Eternal, he fears no more for ever. Nor does this afflict him: What righteousness have I not worked? What evil have I worked? He who thus knows, raises himself above these two; he raises himself above these two, who knows thus. This is the Secret Teaching, the Upanishad.

III

Bhrigu, verily, the son of Varuna, drew near to Varuna his father. Master, teach me the Eternal, said he. To him he declared this: Food, life-breath, sight, hearing, mind, voice; he told him: That from which these beings are born, that whereby they live, that to which they go forth, into which they enter and are absorbed, seek thou to understand that, for that is the Eternal.

He brooded in meditation. When he had brooded in meditation, he understood that the Eternal is food; for from food, verily, these beings are born; born, they live through food; to food they go forth, into it they enter and are absorbed.

When he had understood this, he again drew near to Varuna his father. Master, teach me the Eternal, said he. He told him: Through brooding meditation seek thou to understand the Eternal, for the Eternal is brooding meditation.

He brooded in meditation. When he had brooded in meditation, he understood that the Eternal is life; for from life, verily, these beings are born; born, they live through life; to life they go forth, into it they enter and are absorbed.

When he had understood this, be again drew near to Varuna his father. Master, teach me the Eternal, said he. He told him: Through brooding meditation seek thou to understand the Eternal, for the Eternal is brooding meditation.

He brooded in meditation. When he had brooded in meditation, he understood that the Eternal is mind; for from mind, verily, these beings are born; born, they live through mind; to mind they go forth, into it they enter and are absorbed.

When he had understood this, he again drew near to Varuna his father. Master, teach me the Eternal, said he. He told him: Through brooding meditation seek thou to understand the Eternal, for the Eternal is brooding meditation.

He brooded in meditation. When he had brooded in meditation, he understood that the Eternal is understanding; for from understanding, verily, these beings are born; born, they live through understanding; to understanding they go forth, into it they enter and are absorbed.

When he had understood this, he again drew near to Varuna his father. Master, teach me the Eternal, said he. He told him: Through brooding meditation seek thou to understand the Eternal, for the Eternal is brooding meditation.

He brooded in meditation. When he had brooded in meditation, he understood that the Eternal is joy; for from joy, verily, these beings are born; born, they live through joy; to joy they go forth, into it they enter and are absorbed.

This, verily, is the wisdom of Bhrigu, son of Varuna; in the supreme shining ether it is set firm. He who thus knows, stands firm; possessing food, he becomes the eater of food; he becomes mighty through offspring, through herds, through the radiance of the Eternal, mighty in renown.

Let him not blame food; this is the law. For food is life; the body is the eater of food. In life the body is set firm; in the body life is set firm; therefore, in food, food is set firm. He who knows this food set firm in food, he indeed stands firm; possessing food, he becomes the eater of food; he becomes mighty through offspring, through herds, through the radiance of the Eternal, mighty m renown.

Let him not disregard food; this is the law. For the waters are food; the radiance is the eater of food. In the waters the radiance is set firm; in the radiance the waters are set firm; therefore, in food, food is set firm. He who knows this food set firm in food, he indeed stands firm; possessing food, he becomes the eater of food; he becomes mighty through offspring, through herds, through the radiance of the Eternal, mighty in renown.

Let him make food abundant; this is the law. For the earth is food; shining ether is the eater of food. In the earth, shining ether is set firm; in shining ether the earth is set firm; therefore, in food, food is set firm. He who knows this food set firm in food, he indeed stands firm; possessing food, he becomes the eater of food; he becomes mighty through offspring, through herds, through the radiance of the Eternal, mighty in renown.

Let him not refuse any in the dwelling; this is the law. Therefore, by whatever means, let him obtain much food. Food has become a blessing for him, they say. This food, verily, has been prepared in the beginning. For him who seeks, this food is prepared in the beginning. This food, verily, has been prepared in the middle. For him who seeks, this food is prepared in the middle. This food, verily, has been prepared at the end. For him who seeks, this food is prepared at the end; for him who thus knows.

Conserving the voice, gaining and conserving through the forward-breath and the downward-breath, work for the hands, going for the feet, ridding himself of what is rejected: this is the way of wisdom and worship for mankind. Then the way for the bright powers: abounding joy in the rain, power in the lightning, bright life among creatures, shining light among the stars; the forming of beings, the immortal, joy in creative power; in the shining ether, the all. Let him reverence That as the firm foundation; he gains a firm foundation. Let him reverence That as the mighty; he becomes mighty. Let him reverence That as mind; he becomes lord of mind. Let him reverence That as obeisance; to him desires make obeisance. Let him reverence That as the Eternal; he gains the Eternal. Let him reverence That as dying into the Eternal; they who hate him, who contend against him, the enemies of his own household, die around him. He who is here, in man, and he who is there, in the sun, are one.

He who thus knows, going forth from this world, transcends this self formed of food, he transcends this self formed of life-breath, he transcends this self formed of mind, he transcends this self formed of understanding, he transcends this self formed of bliss; entering those realms, going to and fro, possessing food according to his desire, taking form according to his desire, he dwells there singing this holy song:

Splendour! Splendour! Splendour!

I am the food! I am the food! I am the food!

I am the eater of the food! I am the eater of the food! I am the eater of the food!

I am the maker of the song! I am the maker of the song! I am the maker of the song!

I am the firstborn of the Real, before the gods, from the womb of the immortal!

He who gives me, he also guards me!

I, the food, eat the eater of the food!

I have overcome the world!

I am robed in golden light!

This is the Secret Teaching, the Upanishad.

TAITTIRIYA UPANISHAD

PART I: THE LOTUS OF THE TEACHING

Om Bless us Mitra; bless us Varuna; bless us Aryaman; bless us Indra, Vrhaspati; bless us wide-stepping Vishnu. Obeisance to the Eternal; obeisance to thee, Breath; thou art verily the manifested Eternal I will declare thee, the manifested Eternal. I will declare the true. I will declare the real. May that guard me; may that guard the Speaker; may it guard me; may it guard the Speaker.

Om. Peace. Peace. Peace.

We shall declare the teaching: Color, sound; the measure, the force; the word, the expansion; this is called the study of the teaching.

With us is radiance; with us, the shining of the Eternal. Then we shall declare the hidden teaching of unions, in its five qualities: for the worlds, the fires, the wisdoms, the births, the body. These they call the great unions.

So, as to the worlds. Earth is the first form; heaven, the last form; shining ether, their uniting; the great Breath joins them. Thus for the worlds.

Then as to the fires. Earthly fire is the first form; the sun, the last form; the waters, their uniting; the electric fire joins them. Thus for the fires.

Then as to wisdoms. The Master is the first form; he who dwells beside him, the last form; the wisdom, their uniting; the declaring of it joins them. Thus for the wisdoms.

Then as to births. Mother is the first form; Father, the second form; what is born, their uniting; the engendering joins them. Thus for births.

Then as to the body. The lower jaw is the first form; the upper jaw, the last form; voice is their uniting; the tongue joins them. Thus for the body.

These are the great unions. He who knows the great unions thus declared is united with offspring, cattle, the shining of the Eternal, the food and the rest, the heaven world.

He who is the ruler of the hymns, born more immortal than the hymns,—may he Indra enkindle me with wisdom. O bright one, may I become the receptacle of immortality. May my body be vitalized. May my tongue be honey-sweet. May I hear well with both ears.

Thou art the veil of the Eternal, endowed with wisdom. Guard well the wisdom heard by me. May the power that makes the garment of the Self, wide extended, bringing my vestures and cattle, guard me, giving me food and drink; may that power bring me wealth of well-clad flocks. That power I invoke.

May they who serve the Eternal come to me. That power I invoke.

May they who serve the Eternal pervade me. That power I invoke.

May they who serve the Eternal shine forth in me. That power I invoke.

May they who serve the Eternal give me self-control. That power I invoke.

May they who serve the Eternal bring me peace. That power I invoke.

May I become the shining in men. That power I invoke.

May I become better than riches. That power I invoke;

May I come onward to thee, divine wealth. That power I invoke.

May that divine wealth come onward to me. That power I invoke.

In this thousand-branched power, divine wealth, in thee shall I become clean.

As the waters, forward flowing,—as the months, enter the consumer of days,—so may they who serve the Eternal come to me, approaching from all sides. That power I invoke. Thou art our dwelling; shine forth in me; come near to me, Earth, mid-world, heaven,—there are these three names. The son of Mahâchamasa reveals the fourth; it is Mighty, it is Eternal, it is the Self. Its members are the other shining ones.

Earth is this world; the mid-world is the inter-space; heaven is the other world; the Mighty is the Sun. For from this Sun all three worlds draw their might.

Then Earth is fire; the mid-world is the breath; heaven is the sun; the Mighty is the moon. For from the moon the other lights draw their might.

Then Earth is the Rig; the mid-world is the Sama; heaven is the Yajur; the Mighty is the Eternal. For from the Eternal all the Vedas draw their might.

Then earth is the forward-life; the mid-world is the down ward-life; heaven is the distributing-life; the Mighty is the food. For from the food all the lives draw their might.

These verily are these four, fourfold; four names for each of the four. He who knows these, knows the Eternal. All the bright ones bring their offerings to him.

There is this shining ether in the inner being. Therein is this spirit formed of mind, immortal, golden.

Inward, in the palate, the organ that hangs down like a nipple,—this is a birth-place of Indra. And there, where the dividing of the hair turns round, extending upward to the crown of the head.

Earth rests in fire; the mid-world in the breath; heaven in the Sun; the Mighty in the Eternal. He gains royal power over himself, he gains lordship of mind, he is lord of voice, he is lord of the eye, he is lord of hearing, lord of knowledge; then he becomes the Eternal, bodied in shining ether, the real Self, who delights in life, who is mind, who is bliss; whose wealth is immortal peace.

Earth, inter-space, heaven, space, the spaces between; fire, breath, sun, moon, the star-mansions; waters, lesser growths, greater growths, shining ether, the Self,—there in the realm of being.

Then in the realm of the Self. The forward-life, distributing life, downward-life, upward-life, uniting-life; seeing, hearing, mind, voice, touch; skin, flesh, sinew, bone, muscle; having ascertained these divisions, the seer declared: Fivefold, verily, is all this; by the fivefold he enkindles the fivefold.

Om; thus the Eternal is designated. Om; thus is designated the All. Om; thus affirmation is expressed. Command also, they say; thus they command. Om; the Sama hymns sing. Om; thus the hymns of praise proclaim. Om; thus the priest of offerings makes reply. Om; thus the aspiration goes forth in praise. Om; thus he orders the sacrifice of fire. Om; thus says the knower of the Eternal, about to recite the Vedas: May I gain the Eternal. He, verily, gains the Eternal.

Righteousness, study, teaching; truth, study, teaching; fervor, study, teaching; self-control, study, teaching; peacefulness, study, teaching; the fires, study, teaching; the fire-offering, study, teaching; hospitality, study, teaching; humanity, study, teaching; beings, study, teaching; their coming into being, study, teaching; their being, study, teaching.

As to truth, Satyavachas Rathitaras spoke. As to fervor, Taponitya Paurushishti spoke. As to study and teaching, Naka Maudgalya spoke. This is fervor; this, verily, is fervor.

I am as the life of the tree; my glory is like the mountain-top; I am purified in my root; I am immortal, wealth, splendor. I am full of wisdom, immortal, unfading. This is Trishanku's declaration of wisdom.

Teaching him wisdom, the Master thus instructs him who draws near him: Speak truth; fulfill the law; stray not from earnest study; bringing the wealth dear to the Master, cut not off the thread of being. From truth err not; from the law err not; from well-being err not; from strength err not; from study and teaching err not.

Err not from the works for gods and fathers; take on the divinity of the mother; take on the divinity of the father; take on the divinity of the Master; take on the divinity of the guest.

Whatever deeds are blameless, these are to be followed, not others. Whatever deeds we have done well, these are to be followed by thee, not others.

Whatever knowers of the Eternal are more favored than we, thou shalt honor them by giving a resting-place to them; thou shalt give it with faith; thou shalt not give it without faith; thou shalt give it with grace; thou shalt give it with modesty; thou shalt give it with fear; thou shalt give it with learning. And if thou hast doubts about deeds or doubts about conduct, whatever knowers of the Eternal are of sound judgment, attached, unattached, controlled, lovers of the law,—as they would all in these things, so shalt thou act.

And among designations, whatever knowers of the Eternal are of sound judgment, attached, unattached, controlled, lovers of the law,—as they would act in these things, so shalt thou act.

This is the teaching, this the counsel, this the hidden wisdom, this the instruction, this is what is to be followed; this verily is to be followed.

Om. Bless us Mitra; bless us Varuna; bless us Aryaman; bless us Indra, Vrhaspati; bless us wide-stepping Vishnu. Obeisance to the Eternal; obeisance to thee, Breath, thou art verily the manifested Eternal. I have declared thee the manifested Eternal. I have declared the true, I have declared the real. That has guarded me, that has guarded the Speaker. It has guarded me, it has guarded the Speaker.

Om. Peace. Peace. Peace.

COMMENTARY:

FIRST LESSONS IN THE MYSTERIES

In studying these Books of Hidden Wisdom, one is divided between two opinions: Are the truths and intuitions of life that they convey somewhat carefully hidden, so that only by rather close study one may come to an understanding of what they have to teach; or are they, on the contrary, so openly and frankly expressed that no one having any understanding at all of what they teach can possibly fail to comprehend and assimilate them?

Both opinions are probably true. There are passages so clear, so full of light, so "radiantly shining," to use the words of the Upanishads themselves, that no one whose mind has become in any degree a mirror for higher things can fail to catch their light. While, on the other hand, there are passages, not so much of deliberately concealed meaning, as of complex and profound nature, whose full significance can only be perceived in the light of many other passages, each of which catches a ray from one side of the light of truth, so that only by the reunion of all the rays can their truth shine in its fulness.

Nor is the different quality of these two classes of passages left to be decided by pure chance. Nothing could be further from the truth. On the contrary, the passages most full of "radiant shining" contain just the truths that must shine to us first out of the darkness, truths like these: Find the true Self behind the habitual self; the true Self is born not, nor dies, but is immortal, immemorial, ancient; the true Self is the Eternal,—that thou art.

When we have taken these truths home, and made them free holders of our spirits, so that we know them inwardly, by their own light, by the light of that very Self that is the Eternal, then the whole of life slowly and gradually takes on another face; everything round us in this complicated, many colored world begins to acquire a new and different value and significance. We begin at first to guess, and then clearly to see that life is not at all what we believed it to be, what we were told it was, but something quite other; something far more full of young, quickening vigor, and sweeping, tremendous power that we had believed; and as this awakening gathers force without and within us, we begin to guess strange secrets of the building of the worlds, and how they lie wrapped in the Self that is the Eternal.

Only after one has begun to see this new face of the world can one understand at all what has been said about it by others to whom this same shining light has appeared. And it is this understanding itself which is the key to all riddles and mysteries; a key that can neither be stolen nor given away, but which each one must make or win for himself to the best of his power. The greatest truth of all is oneness. A truth that can hardly be communicated, or gained any other way than by a dawning intuition within the soul, an awakening sense of real and intimate unity with all that is.

Yet, in spite of this oneness, life and the world seem wonderfully varied and changing, always and ever mutable, in perpetual ebb and flow. The one, the real, is presenting itself to us in many ways, in varied vestures, under different veils, in constantly changing disguises.

But as it is the eternal One that wears these veils and vestures and disguises, there is a clearly visible oneness running through them all; as an actor has the same gait and figure in many parts. So that we may group the vestures and disguises into series of types, and then compare them together, according to their corresponding degrees of nearness to, or farness from, the infinite simplicity of the One.

By this grouping of the types of veil and disguise that the One wears in manifested existence, we shall gradually build up a conception of the form and character of the universe; a sacred science of things as they are—sacred, because nothing is holier than the real. To this science of things as they are, no one can have access but they who have taken the first step towards seeing things as they are, who have divined the oneness between their real self and the Self of all beings. Therefore every record of this science will be a closed book to all who have not divined this first secret; while it will be increasingly plain to all who share the secret, in proportion to the force and luminousness of their insight.

The Taittiriya Upanishad seems to be some such record of the sacred science. Here and there, there are broken sentences, broken thoughts, half developed comparisons, abruptly interrupted and fragmentary teachings, as if the hand of time or some other despoiler had borne heavily upon the pages of the record, destroying much and hiding much from sight. Yet, though much has been destroyed, much remains, making this Book of Hidden Wisdom a series of light-flashes, calling up the hidden memories in our hearts, leading us to an understanding of things as they are.

Much will become plain, in this school-book of the mysteries, by comparison with other records of the sacred sciences, and, more than all, by comparison with other parts of the Upanishads themselves. One intuition in particular we shall find running all through the teaching, as the great Breath runs through the three worlds. This is the teaching of the manifesting of the Self in a graduated harmony of steps or worlds; a teaching of which very much has been said in commenting on other Upanishads. And this teaching illustrates very well the distinction between open and hidden science, the latter only intelligible to those who have in some degree caught the light of the Self. The simplest form of this teaching is that side of it that refers to the fields of consciousness of the Self: waking, dreaming, dreamlessness, and the fourth, which is no state but the Self itself.

Until the reality, independence, self-existence of the Self is in some degree divined, this teaching is unintelligible. For even the first step of it, the idea that the manifold, waking, outward world is the lowest mode of the Self, can only be comprehended after it is known that the Self is. Till this knowledge of the Self is gained, it will be believed that the outward, waking world is real, self-existent, independent; and that the sense of self-hood in us is an accident of the reality. Then of dreaming. When the Self is known, it is seen that dreaming is but another mode of manifesting of the Self, a mode of consciousness freed from the tyranny of space; and that the external "realities" of waking life are only frozen dreams, to be presently thawed by the spirit which stands above space. Then again, dreamlessness. People would describe it as the vanishing of something; the disappearance of the outward things that made up the two other worlds of waking and dream. It is, in fact, a disappearance of something; but that something is a double unreality, so that dreamlessness is two degrees nearer the Real than waking, and one degree nearer than dream. This initial lesson depends, as we have seen, on the preliminary understanding of the reality of the Self; till that reality is known by first-hand knowledge, the teaching that dreamlessness is a far more vivid reality than waking life will seem mere nonsense and incoherency.

With this initial lesson of the three steps to the Self, the three worlds where the Self shines with divided light, the Taittiriya Upanishad is largely engaged; and, though the opening and closing sentences of this chapter are probably of a different origin and period, the same idea runs through them also. We may illustrate this by saying that the initials of Mitra, Varuna, and Aryaman, taken in reverse order, form the sacred syllable; that Indra and Brihaspati are names of the higher Self of dreamless reality, Indra being the lord of the azure sphere of the sky, and thus the ruler; Brihaspati corresponding to the planet Jupiter, and being, besides, the Teacher of the "bright ones", as Indra is their ruler. Then again "wide-striding" Vishnu, who strides across the firmament in three paces, is the thread-Self who knits the repeated births together, and becomes manifest through the three times and the three worlds. These three steps of Vishnu are, we are told, a myth of the sun; yes, but then the sun is a myth of the Self. Then again it is not hard to discern the meaning of this: "Obeisance to the Eternal; obeisance to thee, Breath; thou art, verily, the manifested Eternal." Being is manifested as life. The Eternal is Being, the great Breath, "he who sleeps in the Mother," is life made manifest in space.

The first sentence of the Upanishad itself, following this benediction, is not less clear, once certain broad intuitions of the Upanishads are seized. The life becomes manifest through form; as sound, through color; as force, through measure; as the expansive power of the Evolver, through the Evolver's "sister and bride," the feminine, passive Word.

Thus the world and the worlds begin to come into being. Then the five unions or collectivities. In each case, there are the three grades or steps to the Self, pervaded by a power or energy of the Self. First the "union" of the three worlds: earth, or waking life; dreamless life or heaven; and, between these two extremes, the mid-world, the dream-world, the mirror-world, reflecting earth from beneath, and heaven from above; the great Breath,—manifested life,—joins them all three, and knits them together.

Then the three fires. Earthly fire, the energy of vital life; the fire in the waters,—the fire of desire in the waters of emotional life; and the sun, the steady light of intuition. All three, modes of the electric fire, the manifested will of the Self.

Then in exact harmony with these, the Master, who has reached dreamless reality, lit by the fire of intuition, stands above the pupil; the teaching is the link; the declaring of it joins them together. The description of the pupil as "he who dwells beside, on the verge of, the Master" is a very graphic and luminous image. The pupil is he who has already passed over the verge into the circle of light that surrounds the Master, and is to that extent a partaker of his light. Here, as always, the Master is the higher Self, or one in whom the higher Self is luminous, who speaks the language of the higher Self, whose will is the power of the higher Self.

Father, Mother, Child; again an admirable figure. Father is heaven; Mother, earth; the Child is the life engendered between them; the riches of the Self, born of the union of these two powers of the Self.

Then the flocks and herds and offspring that belong to him who knows this union; here, as elsewhere, flocks and herds, the wealth of a pastoral people, are mystically used for the mystical wealth of the awakened Self, the "fruits of the spirit." The "children" are new births; blameless "sons" are new births spent in the gaining of wisdom.

Indra who is to enkindle with wisdom, to make us receptacles of immortality, is again the Sky-lord, the higher Self. It is not difficult to divine the meaning of what follows, in the prayer to Indra: "May my body be vitalized, may my tongue be sweet as honey; may I hear well with both ears." This is the tongue that speaks, the ears that hear, in the presence of the Masters, the ministers of new life ruled by the higher Self.

Then follows the long invocation to the higher Self,—the "veil of the Eternal"—who brings the new vestures and the "flocks and herds" of mystic power; this changes to an invocation of those in whom the higher Self is manifest, the "servants of the Eternal."

Exactly such an invocation must be made by the intuition and will; by the will, as motive power and executive force, guided by the intuition as leader and light; or rather by the single power which is at once will and intuition. There must be a steady, selfless determination to become consciously and completely that higher Self which we divine that we really are; to open our windows to the light, our hearts to the power, of that Self; to make the personal self fade away before, and disappear into, the higher Self. The understanding of this we have already; it remains to make it a living reality by the victories of the will; victories to be gained by steady, unrelaxed aspiration and determination. The tyrannous obstacles in time and space must be melted away and overcome; no mere lapse of time can accomplish this, for the illusion of time is one of the very obstacles in the path, and must fade away into the eternal now of the timeless, ever-living Self.

The invocation is again followed by the teaching of three worlds, the three steps to the Self, in another form.

Then comes a very curious and remarkable passage:

"There is this shining ether in the inner being. Therein is this spirit formed of mind, immortal, golden.

"Inward, in the palate, the organ that hangs down like a nipple,—this is the birthplace of Indra.

"And there, where the dividing of the hair turns round, extending upwards to the crown of the head . . ."

To make this quite clear, we should have to touch on the question of the higher vestures of the Self, their intimate connection with the outermost vesture, and the centres or organs in the head through which the higher vestures come into actual relation with the outer, physical vesture; one organ being thus the outer doorway to the mid-world; the other, to the divine world of the causal, intuitional Self. Both doors must be opened from within; after the unity of the Self has been realized. Till this is done, till unity, the supreme talisman of safety, is won, any study of the "doors" is worse than useless.

The rest of the chapter is a series of finger-points along the path of right understanding, toward the comprehension of unity.

TAITTIRIYA UPANISHAD

PART II: THE LOTUS OF THE BLISS ETERNAL

The knower of the Eternal obtains the supreme; therefore this is declared: Real, wisdom, endless is the Eternal; he who knows that, hid in the secret place, in the supreme firmament of the heart, he obtains all desires through the Eternal that is wisdom.

From that, verily, from this Self, shining-ether was brought forth; from shining-ether, breath; from breath, fire; from fire, the waters; from the waters, earth.

From earth, growths; from growths, food; from food, seed; from seed, man.

He verily, this man, is formed of the essence of food. His head is here; his right side, here; his left side, here; this is himself; this is his basis and support.

As this verse declares:

From food, verily, beings are born,—whatsoever beings dwell on the earth; then by food they live, and to food also they go, at the end.

For food is the eldest of beings, therefore it is called the cause of all growth; they all gain food, who worship food as the Eternal.

Food is the eldest of beings, therefore it is called the cause of all growth :—from food, beings are born; when born, they increase by food; beings are eaten and eat; therefore this is called food that is eaten.

But besides this, formed of the essence of food, there is another inner self, life-formed.

By this, that other is filled; and this, verily, is of the nature of man,—according to the manlike nature of that other, this also is of the nature of man.

Of this life-formed self, the forward-life is the head; the distributing-life is the right side; the downward-life is the left side; the ether is the self; the earth, the basis and support.

As this verse declares:

By life, the bright ones live, and men and cattle also; life verily is the life of beings, and therefore it is called the cause of all life.

They verily reach completed life, who worship life as the Eternal.

This, verily, is the embodied, self of that which comes before it.

But besides this, the life-formed, there is another inner self, mind-formed.

By this, that other is filled; and this, verily, is of the nature of man,—according to the manlike nature of that other, this also is of the nature of man.

Of this mind-formed self, the Yajur, verily, is the head; the Rig, the right side; the Sama, the left side; instruction the self; Atharva-Angirasa the basis and support.

As this verse declares:

That from which voices turn back without gaining it, and mind; knowing that bliss of the Eternal, he fears not for evermore.

This, verily, is the embodied self of that which comes before it.

But besides this, the mind-formed, there is another inner self, knowledge-formed.

By this, that other is filled; and this, verily, is of the nature of man,—according to the manlike nature of that other, this also is of the nature of man.

Of this knowledge-formed self, faith is the head; righteousness, the right side; reality is the left side; union is the self; the world-soul is the basis and support.

As this verse declares:

Knowledge draws forth sacrifice, it draws forth works also; knowledge all the bright ones worship, as the eldest, the Eternal.

If he knows knowledge as the Eternal, if he wanders not from this; in the body, putting off all darkness, he attains all his desires.

This, verily, is the embodied self of that which comes before it.

But besides this, the knowledge-formed, there is another inner self, bliss-formed.

By this, that other is filled; and this, verily, is of the nature of man,—according to the manlike nature of that other, this also is of the nature of man.

Of this bliss-formed self, what is dear is the head; joy is the right side; rejoicing, the left side; bliss, the self; the Eternal, the basis and support.

As this verse declares:

Being non-being, verily, this comes into being; he who knows the Eternal as non-being,—if he knows that the Eternal yet really is,—him they know as really being.

This is, verily, the embodied self of what goes before it.

Then there are these questions: whether he who has not attained wisdom, on going forth from this world goes to that world; and whether he who has attained wisdom, on going forth from this world, attains that world.

He formed the desire: Let me become great, let me produce beings. He brooded with fervor; having brooded with fervor, he put forth all this existence, whatsoever exists. Having put forth this, he went forth after it, and entered into it. Having gone forth after it and entered into it, he became the real and the outward; the defined and the undefined; the encompassed and the unencompassed; knowledge and unknowledge; reality and the untrue. He became all that depends on the real, whatsoever there is. Therefore they call this dependent on reality.

As this verse declares

Non-being was this, verily, in the beginning.

Therefrom being was born. This he made as himself. Therefore this is called well made. And as this is well made, therefore it is excellent in essence. He, verily, who has gained this essence, becomes full of bliss. For who would live, who would breathe, if this shining-ether were not bliss? This therefore is the cause of bliss.

For when he finds the fearless, the resting-place in this invisible, selfless, undefined, unencompassed being, then he is one who has gained the fearless.

But he who makes for himself antagonism in this being, for him fear is; fear is his who sees and believes thus.

As this verse declares:

Through fear of that, Breath blows; through fear of that, rises the Sun; through fear of that, Fire and Moon; and Death runs as fifth.

This, therefore, is the measuring of bliss:

Let there be a youth of excellent nature and fully accomplished, well taught, full of firmness and power; let this whole earth be full of riches for him. This is one human bliss.

And if there be a hundred measures of such human bliss, this is one bliss of the celestial singers of human form, or of a sage who has ceased from desire.

And if there be a hundred measures of the bliss of celestial singers of human form, this is one bliss of the divine celestial singers, or of a sage who has ceased from desire.

And if there be a hundred measures of the bliss of divine celestial singers, this is one bliss of the fathers who dwell in the long-lasting world, or of a sage who has ceased from desire.

And if there be a hundred measures of the bliss of the fathers who dwell in the long-lasting world, this is one bliss of the divine beings born in the birth-world, or of a sage who has ceased from desire.

And if there be a hundred measures of the bliss of the divine beings born in the birth-world, this is one bliss of the divine formative beings,—those who through works ascend to the divine beings,—or of a sage who has ceased from desire.

And if there be a hundred measures of the bliss of the divine formative beings, this is one bliss of the pure divine beings, or of the sage who has ceased from desire.

And if there be a hundred measures of the bliss of the pure divine beings, this is one bliss of the Sky-lord Indra, or of the sage who has ceased from desire.

And if there be a hundred measures of the bliss of the Sky-lord Indra, this is one bliss of the great lord of Vrhaspati, or of the sage who has ceased from desire.

And if there be a hundred measures of the bliss of the great lord Vrhaspati, this is one bliss of the lord of beings, Prajapati, or of the sage who has ceased from desire.

And if there be a hundred measures of the bliss of the lord of beings, Prajapati, this is one bliss of the Eternal, or of the sage who has ceased from desire.

And the power that is here, in man, and the power that is there, in the sun, is one and the same.

He who knows thus, on going forth from this world reaches and is united with the self formed of the essence of food; he reaches and is united with the life-formed self; he reaches and is united with the mind-formed self; he reaches and is united with the knowledge-formed self; he reaches and is united with the bliss-formed self.

As this verse declares:

That from which voices turn back without reaching it, and mind also,—knowing that bliss of the Eternal, he fears nothing any more.

This thought no longer burns in him:

What have I not done well, what have I done ill?

He who knows thus, embraces them as Self; he embraces them both as Self, who knows thus. Thus the Book of Hidden Wisdom.

COMMENTARY:

THE FIVE VEILS OF THE SELF

Who could live, who could breathe, if that shining-ether were not bliss?

This sentence strikes the note of the teaching, that has been called the Lotus of the bliss of the Eternal.

It contains two distinct chapters or phases of those instructions which are spoken of as following and crowning the four Vedas. The first phase is the teaching of emanations; the second is the teaching of the five veils of the Self, or, as they are called here, the five inner selves. But, by some accident of memory or arrangement, the second part of the teaching of emanation has been divided from the first by a long intervening section on the five veils, which, again, is separated by a section on cosmogony, from the verses that form its legitimate conclusion. This separation and intermingling of incongruous material is, perhaps, the result of accident; perhaps the result of design,—a simple expedient to turn away at the outset students whose sole motive is curiosity, or who "having no depth of earth" will bear only a swiftly growing, swiftly withering crop of good intentions.

But if this be the design, it is so transparent that one needs only to rearrange the sections to give the teaching perfect sequence and lucidity. First, the teaching of emanations.

"Being unmanifest, verily, That comes into manifestation; he who knows the Eternal as unmanifest, and yet knows that the

Eternal is, him they know as really being. . . . He formed the desire: let me become great, let me produce beings. He brooded with fervor. Having brooded with fervor, he put forth all this, whatsoever exists. Having put forth this, he went forth after it, and entered into it.

"From this Self, verily, shining-ether was brought forth; from shining-ether, breath; from breath, fire; from fire, the waters; from the waters, earth; From earth, growths; from growths, food; from food, seed; from seed, man."

Here, as everywhere in the Books of Hidden Wisdom, there is a very clear sevenfold classification; the seven outward stages of manifestation: The Eternal, Manifestation or the Voice, Ether, Air, Fire, Waters, Earth.

Then again, a return along these stages back toward the unmanifested; with Man as the fifth stage of the homeward journey.

Then the second division of this chapter, the teaching of the five veils of the Self, or the five inner selves; again requiring the paragraphs to be arranged, and no more, in order to make the instructions perfectly clear, regular, and symmetrical. The five veils are described thus:

"First, the inner self formed of the essence of food,"—the form of the body of man. It is clearly not the physical body, for, later on, we are told that, on "going forth" from the physical body, the man first reaches and is united with this inner self of the essence of food. This "going forth" has evidently two meanings, here as elsewhere; it is either the upward return of death, after a single life, or it is the far greater upward return, after the whole circle of births and rebirths;

the great upward return to the Eternal, along the "small old path, stretching far away; the path that the sages tread," as another Book of Hidden Wisdom calls it.

Then, after this form of the body of man, comes the next veil of the Self, the next inner self:

"The life-formed self; by this life-formed self the form of the body is filled; it is also of the shape of man,—according to the manlike shape of the other, this is also of the shape of man."

This vital self or vital veil contains the five-fold life: the upward-life, uniting-life, forward-life, distributing-life, downward-life. And this vital self is the self embodied in the preceding formal self.

Then above this vital self, and embodied in it, comes the emotional self or the mind-formed self, as it is here called; the veil of the impulses that set the vital forces in action.

The comparison of these impulses with the four Vedas and the secret instructions as fifth, is not so fanciful as it at first sight seems, because the songs, hymns, chants, and charms of the Vedas were considered as impulses and forces, set in motion by the worshippers, and impelling the "gods" to bring to the worshippers a desired return in the form of some satisfaction or gratification. These gratifications, in far the greater number of cases, were "sons, grandsons of a hundred years, horses and elephants and gold;" the chief utility of the sons and grandsons being to pray their progenitor into paradise, and keep him there by the force of their yearly rites.

Therefore the comparison of the Vedic songs and chants and charms with the impulses of the body of desire is far more just than a first glance shows. As before, this self of impulse is embodied in the vital self that precedes it.

Within this self of impulse, again, another inner self is embodied; the knowledge-formed self, the knowledge-formed veil of the self. It is the knowing, apprehending part of man; the part that stands above the impulses, and gradually comes to comprehend their meaning, direction, and tendency, so that, in due time, these impulses and forces may be turned to the purposes of of the Self. The five elements of this inner self, as understood by the teachers of this book of hidden wisdom, are: faith, righteousness, reality, union, the approach to the world-soul. They make up the inner sense of the trueness of things and the real values of things; and especially the sense of the truth that the self is one with the Self; that the individual is one with the Supreme. The end of this knowledge, we are told, is the putting off of all darkness while in the body, so that, on going forth, the Eternal may be attained. This knowledge-formed self is embodied in the self that precedes it,—the self of impulse and desire.

Within, above it, is the bliss-formed self, whose parts are joy, gladness, rejoicing and bliss; whose proper home is the Eternal. From the Supreme Self it is divided only by the thinnest vesture of illusion, the illusion of separateness from the Eternal.

Then the five veils: formal, vital, impulsive, intellectual, spiritual. They very evidently correspond with the form, vitality, body of desire, mind, and soul, of another sevenfold classification;

but their relation to the more usual threefold or fourfold division of the Upanishads is not so immediately evident.

This threefold division that has already been examined at great length is of course that of the three fires, the three vestures, the three selves, the three worlds.

Taking the last, the three worlds, we find that they are often spoken of as earth, mid-world and heaven; or again, as earth, the waters, and radiance; or, yet again, as waking, dreaming, and dreamless intuition.

How, then, are the five veils of the Self, the five-inner selves of the present teaching, to be correlated with these three worlds so often found in other teachings? Apparently in this way: to the outermost of the three worlds belongs one veil; to the innermost also one; to the midmost, three, Of these three, the lower is a reflection of the outermost world in the waters, from below; while the higher is a reflection of the highest world, from above. Thus the formal body, the formal veil, of the fivefold series belongs to the lowest and outermost of the three worlds,—earth, or waking, physical life.

The vital body is a reflection of this in the mid-world, the mirror-world of the "waters;" it shares the nature of the world of the "waters" in the ebb and flow of vital life; it bears the imprint and reflection of the outermost world, as "after the manlike shape of the formal body it has a manlike shape."

The emotional, mental veil, the mind-formed, the body of desire, is most characteristic of the mid-world, the world of the waters, and shares its proper nature. Like the waves and currents of the waters, the impulses ebb and flow, rise and fall, flow this way and that; and this fugitive, fleeting nature of theirs is very well brought out in the philosophical definition of mind. "What is mind?" it is asked, in Shankara's Catechism; and the answer is, "Mind is that which intends and doubts;—which builds together and unbuilds again,"—to give the words their strictest and most simple meaning. It is, of course, clear that this is a quite different use of the word "mind," from that which would identify it with spirit; so that, perhaps, it would be better invariably to use some word like emotion or impulse, which really build up and unbuild again, and to avoid the word "mind" altogether.

Then the knowledge-formed veil, also belonging to the middle world, but being a reflection in it of the pure intuition of the third and divine world above; this makes up the three veils that belong to the mid-world of the waters, of dream, of fluid life; one reflected from below, one from above, one between these two.

To the divine world belongs the last veil, the bliss-formed; because bliss is part of the proper nature of the divine world, as are also eternity and wisdom; the opposite of these, misery, death, ignorance, being no more than abnormal, unnatural departures from the divine world, and exclusions of the divine world.

Separated by "the measuring of bliss" from the rest of the teaching of the five veils, stands a paragraph, whose true place is clearly immediately after the teaching of the veils, in answer to the questions as to those "who have gone forth," and the worlds they reach.

"He who knows this, on going forth, reaches successively and is united with the formal self, the vital self, the emotional self, the intellectual self, the blissful self".

The "measuring of bliss" seems to embody a teaching of the worlds above the human world, and the lives and dwellers therein; it may well be compared with the Buddhist teaching on the same question, that follows the teaching of the Noble Eightfold Path.

Then the conclusion of this, as of every teaching, the divine Self "from which voice turns back, and mind also, without reaching it; knowing that bliss of the Eternal, he fears nothing any more."

TAITTIRIYA UPANISHAD

PART III: THE LOTUS OF THE SAGE BHRGU

Invocation

Om. May That guard us two—teacher and pupil; may That save us two; may we two do the work with valor; may we be full of radiance; may the lesson be well learned; may no discord arise to separate us. Om. Peace; Peace; Peace.

Bhrgu was Varuna's son; he came up to his father Varuna: Master, teach me the Eternal, said he.

The world-food, the breath, the seeing, the hearing, mind, the voice,—he answered him,—That from which these beings are born, That by which when born they live, That to which they go forward and enter it completely, try to find out That for yourself,—That is the Eternal.

He brooded fervently; and, brooding fervently, he thought: the world-food is the Eternal; for it is exactly from the world-food that these beings are born; by the world-food, when born, they live; the world-food they go forward to and enter it completely. And, thinking thus, he again came up to his father Varuna: Master, teach me the Eternal, said he. The Master answered him: try to find out the Eternal for yourself by brooding fervently, for the Eternal is fervent brooding.

He brooded fervently; and, brooding fervently, he thought: the breath is the Eternal; for it is exactly from the breath that these beings are born; by breath, when born, they live; breath they go forward to, and enter into it completely. And, thinking thus, he again came up to his father Varuna: Master, teach me the Eternal, said he. The Master answered him: try to find out the Eternal for yourself by brooding fervently, for the Eternal is fervent brooding.

He brooded fervently, and, brooding fervently, he thought: mind is the Eternal; for it is exactly from mind that these beings are born; by mind, when born, they live; mind they go forward to, and enter it completely. And, thinking thus, he again came up to his father Varuna: Master, teach me the Eternal, said he. The Master answered him: Try to find out the Eternal for yourself by brooding fervently, for the Eternal is fervent brooding.

He brooded fervently, and, brooding fervently, he thought: the soul that knows is the Eternal; for it is exactly from the soul that knows that these beings are born; by the soul that knows, when born, they live; the soul that knows, they go forward to, and enter it completely. And, thinking thus, he again came up to his father Varuna: Master, teach me the Eternal, said he. The Master answered him: Try to find out the Eternal for yourself by brooding fervently, for the Eternal is fervent brooding.

He brooded fervently; and, brooding fervently, he thought; Bliss is the Eternal; for it is exactly from bliss that these beings are born; by bliss, when born, they live; bliss they go forward to, and enter it completely.

This is that teaching of the sage Bhrgu the son of Varuna; this stands firm in the supreme holy ether. He who knows thus, stands firm. Possessing the world-food, he becomes a consumer of the world-food. He becomes mighty through offspring, flocks, radiance of the Eternal, mighty in renown.

Let him not reproach the world-food; this is the sacred vow. For the breath is verily the world-food; the body is a consumer of the world-food; in the breath the body rest firmly; in the body the breath rests firmly. Thus the world-food rests firmly in the world-food. He who knows the world-food thus resting firmly in the world-food, himself stands firm. Possessing the world-food, he becomes an eater of the world-food; he becomes mighty through offspring, flocks, radiance of the Eternal, mighty in renown.

Let him not overlook the world-food; this is the sacred vow. For the waters verily are the world-food; the fire is a consumer of the world-food; in the waters the fire rests secure; in the fire the waters rest secure; thus the world-food rests secure in the world-food. He who thus knows the world-food resting secure in the world-food, he himself rests secure. Possessing the world-food, he becomes an eater of the world-food; he becomes mighty through offspring, flocks, radiance of the Eternal, mighty in renown.

Let him magnify the world-food; this is the sacred vow. For the earth is the world-food; the shining ether is a consumer of the world-food; in the earth the shining ether rests secure. In the shining ether the earth rests secure; thus the world-food rests securely in the world-food. He who thus knows the world-food resting secure in the world-food, he becomes an eater of the world-food; he becomes mighty through offspring, flocks, radiance of the Eternal, mighty in renown.

Let him not refuse to any a part in the habitation; this is the sacred vow. Therefore, by whatever practice, let a man gain the world-food abundantly. The world-food has been made ready for him,—thus they say. This world-food has, verily, been made ready from the head; from the head for him it is made ready. This world-food has, verily, been made ready from the middle; from the middle for him it is made ready. This world food has, verily, been made ready from the end, from the end, verily, for him it is made ready.

He who knows thus: as power, this is in the voice; as possessions, in the forward breath and downward breath; as work, in the hands; as going, in the two feet; as putting forth in the power that puts forth; these are the human names of That. Then as to the names of the shining powers: as fulness, this is in the rain; as force, in the lightning; as well-being, in the flocks; as light, in the houses of the stars; as lord of being, immortality and bliss, in the power that generates; as the all in the shining ether.

Let him draw near, saying: this is the secure resting place. He gains a secure resting place.

Let him draw near, saying: this is the mighty. He becomes mighty.

Let him draw near, saying: this is mind. He becomes possessed of mind.

Let him draw near, saying: this is the power that bends. His desires are bent before him.

Let him draw near, saying: this is the Eternal. He becomes full of the Eternal.

Let him draw near, saying: this is the Eternals destroying power. His enemies who dwell within his house are destroyed, and the Sons of his brothers who are not dear to him.

The power that is here in the spirit, and the power that is there in the sun—that power is one.

He who thus knows—on going forth from this world, he departs toward, and reaches, the self formed of the world-food;

He departs toward, and reaches, the self formed of breath;

He departs toward, and reaches, the self formed of mind;

He departs toward, and reaches, the self formed of the soul that knows:

He departs toward, and reaches, the self formed of bliss. Passing through these worlds, possessing the world-food according to his desire, taking forms according to his desire, he dwells there, singing this song of oneness.

Wonder, wonder, wonder; I am the world-food, I am the world food, I am the world-food;

I am the eater of the world-food, I am the eater of the world-food, I am the eater of the world-food.

I am the maker of the song, I am the maker of the song, I am the maker of the song.

I am the first born of the true;

Before the shining powers, in the heart of the immortal.

He who gives me the world-food, he verily preserves me here;

I, as the world-food, destroy him who gives not the world-food

I have perfectly become all that is;

I am full of golden light; he who thus knows—

Thus the teaching of hidden wisdom.

Invocation

May That guard us two; may That save us two; may we two do the work with valor; may we be full of radiance; may the lesson be well learned; may no discord arise to separate us.

Om. Peace; Peace; Peace.

Bless us Mitra; bless us Varuna; bless us Aryaman; bless us Indra, Vrhaspati; bless us wide-stepping Vishnu. Obeisance to the Eternal; obeisance to thee, Breath; Thou art verily the manifested Eternal. I will declare thee, the manifested Eternal. will declare the true. I will declare the real. May that guard me. May that guard the speaker. May it guard me. May it guard the speaker.

Om. Peace; Peace; Peace.

COMMENTARY:

THE FOOD OF THE WORLD

The third part of this Book of Hidden Wisdom, like the first two, thoroughly suggests to us that it is a manual or first lesson-book for students of the mysteries, or rather a series of fragments from an old lesson-book, mutilated either by the hand of time or the hand of the restrictor of knowledge. It is to be studied by the teacher and pupil together; this is the meaning of the invocation: "May That, the nameless Eternal, guard us two; may we be full of radiance; may no discord arise to keep us apart."

For there can be no teaching until the pupil has thought and lived himself into the spirit of the master; no beginning of the teaching until the pupil finds himself already doing, though with imperfect light, the same great work that the master has already long been doing with valor and perfect wisdom.

The lesson here is the parable of an ideal teacher and his pupil; a form of teaching used everywhere through these books, as where Death teaches Nachiketas; where the kingly sage teaches Uddalaka; where Uddalaka teaches his son; where Pippalada teaches his six pupils. The teacher, the higher Self, or one in whom the higher Self is absorbed, and brightly shining; the pupil, the habitual self, reaching up toward the higher Self, and striving, above all things, to let no discord keep him apart from the higher Self.

Here the teacher is Varuna, the old god of the ocean of space; the pupil, the sage Bhrigu, after whom the whole section of teaching is named. The teacher answered his appeal for wisdom thus: "That from which the five outward elements are born, whereby they live, where again they return, that is the Eternal;—try to find it but for yourself."

The pupil, following this excellent counsel, set himself to find out the Eternal for himself; he made his thought flow outwards to the world without him, then return within him, to become conscious of its own being; he let the Self which is wisdom do its own work in the secret place of the heart; or, to use the quaint phrase of the old book, he brooded fervently.

The world-food, he thought, must be the Eternal; the wonderfull stuff, whatever it be, that pictorial outer things are built up of; the substance of the sun and stars, the mountains and rivers, the sky and sea.

But the master sent him back again to learn the lesson, neither saying that this world-food, the strange substance of outward things, is the Eternal, nor that it is not the Eternal. His answer drove the pupil again within himself, and withdrawing again to the secret place of the heart, he grew to feel that that strange substance of outward things and appearances is not the all in all; that there are other powers moving this and breathing through it; or, in the words we are used to, that matter is not a reality, a thing in itself, but only the hiding place of force; that the atoms of matter are not absolute, but only centres of force. But we will keep to the old picturesque speech of Bhrigu; the world-food is not all; there is the breath that lives and breathes through the world-food; the breath must be the Eternal.

Again the Master, neither denying nor affirming, sent the pupil back to brood once more within himself. Growing more vividly conscious within, he saw that this vivid emotion and feeling of his were a greater reality even than the breath; that they were nearer to him, known at first hand, while the world-food and the breath were known only outwardly, at second hand, known only through his own vivid emotion and feeling. This vivid feeling, mind, he thought, must be the Eternal.

Again sent back by the Master, he saw that even feeling and mind are more outward than the soul within him that perceives them, and this soul that perceives, he thought, must be the Eternal.

At last, by a happy inspiration, he discovered the teaching to which the master had been leading him: Bliss is the Eternal; the Eternal is Bliss. The one reality is the Self that is Bliss, self-being, self-subsisting, self-satisfying, the fulness of all things forever. The one pain is deprivation, separation, antagonism: but in the one Self that is the All, there can be no deprivation, no separation, no antagonism, no pain; only perfect Bliss for ever.

Thus the teaching of Bhrigu; and one can hardly imagine a better and happier way of picturing the onward path of life, where each advance is marked by the appearance of a new self and a new world; not confounding and destroying the old, but transforming them, illumining them, penetrating them with a life that makes all things new.

Then follow a series of admonitions, to establish the learning soul in the right way. Let him not reproach the world-food; let him not turn back in bitter asceticism from the great outward pictorial world; for it is the garment of the Self, woven by the breath for the purposes of the Self. Let him not reject and spurn life, but rather gladly accept and learn its admirable wealth. For the divine world-food,—the Self,—rests firmly in the outer world-food,—the pictorial universe,—and the whole of the universe is to be made radiant and breathing by the Self, till it becomes one with the Self, till nothing is but the Self.

Let him not refuse to any a part in the habitation; for all selves are his other selves; rays from the one Self that is his own truest Self.

The powers of the Self lie hid in all things, in voice, breath, hands; in cloud, lightning, fire. Let him draw near and become possessed of them. And there is the destroying power of the Self that is to destroy the enemies of the Self, deprivation and separation and antagonism; these are the enemies who dwell within his house; they are the sons of his false brothers,—the children of the lower selves of passion and hate that usurp the place of the one true Self.

When all the children of separation are destroyed, he becomes one with the Self, the Self that is the world, and dwells there, singing the song of oneness, knowing himself to be the breath within the world-food, the inventor of the game of life, the maker of the song: I am the first born of the true; born in the heart of the immortal, before the shining powers; I have perfectly become all that is; I am full of golden light.

www.ingramcontent.com/pod-product-compliance
Lightning Source LLC
LaVergne TN
LVHW041458070426
835507LV00009B/665